At the Town Café

To the memory of my mother.

At the Town Café

Poetry of

Cat Kigerl

Goldfish Press
Seattle

Published by
Goldfish Press, Seattle

2012 18th Avenue South
Seattle, WA 98144

Manufactured in the United States of America

ISBN - 13: 978-0978797553
ISBN - 10: 0978797558

Library of Congress Catalog Card Number 2016906146

Acknowledgements: I am grateful to Koon Woon and Goldfish Press
for this book, to Joe Greer for his poet-proofreader's eye and to my
husband, William with whom I continue to share life's truths.

Cover Photo: Cat Kigerl

Table of Contents

A Delicate Unfolding

Last of ebb, and daylight waning. —*Walt Whitman*

It is the early mornings I know best
now
in the atmosphere of a certain age
unwinding
like a bolt of cloth around time
sometimes constricting.

The smell of the sea, shellfish, oily,
seeps up from the bay
bits of light not yet ascending.
Daylight stalls in these moments,
resistant
to the change, from darkness to light.

It is a delicate unfolding
a pause before the leap
the drawing in of the night's breath
then letting it out slowly.

The water circles somewhere in tiny eddies
disturbed by an unseen form
before it smoothes again.

The little disturbances
in the burgeoning light.

We do not know

We do not know how long
we are here
as the wind blows,
the water tosses
with facsimiles of the seasons
like the grasshoppers short stint
in a fast-paced autumn,
the apples not yet fallen,
the ducks not yet tucked inside the harbor,
November creeping in fast,
coyote's rushing through the field,
dragonflies hovering for one day, then gone.
All within a year's passing
on the backseat of mind.

Students, colleagues, professors,
get filed away,
while the tree rises higher each year.
Like Eliot's bedded axel-tree
the turning wheel rolls forward and nothing stays,
be it Frost's gold or
the hardy maple leaf as big as a hand,
slanting to the ground.

In the Teak-Tinted Light

What is it about the constancy
of passing days, of each morning's arrival
with its cloudy skies
its non-promise about tomorrow
in the teak-tinted light?

There in the tranquility
of the tree-shrouded shore
old fancies swaying in an imagined wind
the fluty chorus of morning birds
announcing a hidden sun
edging into the passing moments.

A Train Whistle in the Night

Part I

My mother has entered
the age of fragility,
a time when the hands
have lost a firm grip to the wont of gnarled knuckles,
a time when the eyesight has become so dim
that the mind, without a picture to hold a thought,
strays
away from a question
no matter how many times it is repeated
over
again.
It is a time when new memories
are as fleeting
as a train whistle in the night,
skirting around the synapses like so many bends in the tracks
the rails twisting.
But it is also a time of vivid clarity
when old times,
a trip home in the 1940's, the camera a brother left behind
before he was killed in the war,
are still recalled as quickly, with as much longing,
as the steps to a home-style jig.

It is a time when the footfall, just short of the stair,
can potentially be
for she who once prided herself on style,
as catastrophic
as not being able to see
which two socks make a pair
and which two do not,
when the classy perfume she once shared
was it Chanel?
has withered down to a nostalgic scent
like a dish of dried roses
left on the windowsill too long.
And the shoes,

those calve-shaping high-heeled shoes
worn proudly into her 80's every Sunday
are now stored tightly in cardboard boxes
while the dresses of rayon, cotton or silk,
in so many shades of blue,
still her favorite color
are now cloistered in garment bags
with the essence of moth balls
in the hush of a darkened closet.

Part II

Her words are sometimes but a few
over the telephone wires
at times lucid with wisdom,
at other times vague
when she confuses you with your aunt
and you speak the part as though you are.
But the tone of her voice,
familiar feelings tunneled inside,
is still crystal clear
despite the misfiring, the cognitive change.

She never expected to live this long,
long enough to know
a husband's laundering, cooking, dishwashing
after decades of her servitude.
Was it her destiny
to give him time
to rise to a state of caring
for the delicate details
of a wife's 94 years?
Was it to find out
after her death a year later in an Adult Care Home,
that longevity
becomes a timeless learning
and waking life
can be as fleeting as dream?

I envy the Great Horned Owl

I envy the Great Horned Owl
for his seclusion,
for his trusted position at the old barn entrance,
a sentinel at a remote post
sweeping over our path silently
in surveillance.
I admire his perch on a barren oak tree,
hiding his bulk between limbs,
transparent to all who seek him.

In the silence of rotting wood
at high noon,
in the gentle creaking of boards atrophying,
I envy his patience
with the absent scurry of a blind mouse
admitted only by the timing of the owl's craft.

The slow hours turn to afternoon,
a moon shuffles slowly into the wake of his sanctuary
and I admire his resilience amidst the haunting
of so many tiny feet pursuing his psyche at night-watch.

The Wind is Blowing in Weed
California

I. Autumn
It is kicking sand into the eyes
of the orange dog
that tries to sleep on the side of the road
next to a flatbed truck
and makes him raise his head
and drop it once again.

It is sneaking through
the worn seams
of the tie-dyed t-shirt
the old hippie wears
as he carries his rucksack
of clothes
into the laundromat.

It tries to push down
the boards
graying with age
of the cedar fence
that surrounds the old mill
workers house
and shakes the rickety gate
next to the mailbox
one more time.

It sweeps over the onion trucks
passing through town
on a break from the Interstate
tumbling onions to the ground
then weaves through the new-cut logs
stacked like a giants' kindling
on a logging truck
that whizzes toward
a mill yard
Abner Weed

established
in 1901
along with the town.

The wind is threatening a cold winter
by taking a big bite
from the memory of summer
in the middle of the night
as it races over the parked cars
leaving a thin cake of ice
on all the windshields.

The train inches along the tracks.
With a long blast, it parts the wind,
overtaking its vigor
until it disappears around the hill
and beyond.

The air pauses on my street.
Then the wind
blows again
making the cedar needles skitter
across my veranda
like little mouse feet.

II. Winter

The wind is blowing the snow
and like heaps of sand in a desert
the snow drifts
become great dunes.
It swirls the snow into eddies
and I think of water.
Only this wind-driven snow is soft and dry
and as light as sparrow feathers
as it floats to the ground.

The wind in Weed
is an ancient wind
and retraces its steps

along desolate hills,
carving their borders
deeper, monitoring their boundaries
like it has for millions of years
while I, huddled inside
by the heat,
wonder if I've settled in a cavern
on Mars.

It is howling along the contours
of the house,
thrusting its breath into the siding
and like a pack of coyotes
it quiets momentarily,
pacing,
while it seeks a hollow entry
hungry for the warmth inside.
The wind in Weed
is a constant wind
but never stays long.
Soon the snow is disintegrating
but the wind lays in waiting
for the next season
so that it can feed
the town its fury
once again.

III. Spring
The wind is waiting
beyond the mountain
while the rest of the elements
shift from winter
to summer,
snow flurries to sunshine,
and back again
in one week
until winter reluctantly
gives up and flies
north.

The wind offers a few gusts
on an afternoon of clouds,
promising to drive force
into a spring rain,
then recedes so the sun can take charge
and bring ants scurrying out of their holes,
marching
up the shingles of houses
and through windowsills
unsealed by the winter wind.
The sun begins to parch
exposed skin
and the wind bides its time
not uttering a word
while the town jumps ahead,
bypassing spring
for summer.

IV. Summer

The wind is barely blowing now
and the town is melancholy
in the slow warm of summer,
the old saw mill
its faded green walls
is wistful on the edge of a silent yard
piled with wood scrap
and old sawdust,
its entrance dark
like a mouth agape
a draft wheezing through
the rafters like the ghosts
of saw mill workers calling to one another
in the heyday of production.
The railroad tracks leading to the mill are overgrown
with grass and stretch into bushes
and tangles.
Down the line a cricket disturbs
the emptiness

and tries to chirp hope but the sadness
clinging to its hind legs tells only that night is coming on soon.

The streets in the town are grey and quiet
for the wind seldom idles here now
and the old orange dog slumps down
in the middle of the dusty road
in the sunshine of late afternoon
his head on his paws, half waiting
to be disturbed
by the feral cats who ensure few birds
sing at morning, few mice scratch at doors,
sashaying cats, the only thing growing in numbers.

The wind, like the mill, is a trademark of the past
until the solstice turns and the long days pull
like boxcars into autumn when the wind
will tear around the mountain
and surprise the town,
uprooting its namesake
and blowing seeds adrift.

The Bones of the Headlands
Point Cabrillo, California

The bones of the headlands
are carved by the blood of the sea,
each corner a jagged change
of time
as land turns back
to leeward
like a confusion of abstract puzzle pieces
side-winding in space,
lands of the periphery,
supine.

The headlands speak of eons
and the opposites hide inside their hard shell.
In a womb of the forlorn,
an infant crust of dirt and stone
marks the grave of these headlands
and like an old man on bent knee,
they contemplate the past.
The yin and yang
of the crawling and the crashing
waves below
speaks for the moment,
and steady's the hand
of land and land not.

The gull knows the forces, the faces of these bones.
He knows false security in tufts of loam,
wet from rains, bitter cold
unwelcome to webbed foot,
while the ocean squelches, the sun stabs his moot
hunt. But the gull forgives and forages,
his belly as lead.

Like an earthly corpse
the elements have scoured, sculpted these bones, these legs

and lands
now grass and heather-covered
sinews porous, the marrow crusted and old
yet still a hint of fresh tucked inside.
The bones roast
under the sun's lamp
to eventually spin into dust.

Water, wind and land are the headland's song.
The gull, the piper trill it on the wind.
The song's low octave is the sea's surf,
the purple lupine harmonizing as color.
The moon, bright on a settled night,
drums it in its pull.
The headland's place of rest,
is where earth-forms,
alive, dead,
hold count with time and timelessness.
Such notions
of shared beauty
find their youth
and winsomeness
of new sprout
in the land's slow call.

The land bows
to land.

Subject are the headlands,
yet as still
as 'forgotten in time.'

The Marrow of the Inlands
Klamath River, California

The marrow of the inlands
quintessential life
beat at the heart
of a rim-rock,
curved like the spine of a dinosaur's back,
summoning, guarding
the river from within
as it dances
delicately,
sweeping its dress
around cliff's edges
like a bride.

Sage-blessed,
pumping silently inside a mineral throne,
in a millenniums-long kingdom,
generously receiving the summer rains,
capturing the water, depositing it for late season feed,
offering a slow drink to flora and fauna not bred to survive
famine. Benevolent is this marrow,
dutiful,
carefully disguised by inland bones. *(Are they fossilized?)*
Knowing
life nourishes life
under the veiled soil.

Images, Reflections, Questions. On Fisherman's Harbor. *Washington*

This is the fallow season
when winter has penetrated the hollows
of tree trunk and dormant seed.
The apple tree bare in the waning sunlight
tries to boast of three bright red fruits
hanging on like ornaments on an abandoned Christmas tree.
The wild grasses fold into bundles
hunkering in the icy wind.
On the harbor the ducks are at ease
floating past time
within TS Eliot's eternal present,
skirting the water
as it flattens in late afternoon.

On a Saturday morning the harbor sleeps in
like a mirage, an illusion
it waits for a still hand
to dab at a color
paint the inner filaments
the details of pine needle and leaf
transposed in seconds of dawning light.
To watch the fluid shifting
of an early morning
is to also see it in one's self
constant increments embedded in the mystery
that which compresses it all
diamond-hard,
softer than vapor
a song in the night.

High in the sky a blackbird flies.
A string on the filament,
he leaves a trace of himself
only on the viewers mind
like the traces of snow patterning the ground
in hollow spaces, melting.

This harbor is a haven, a refuge
for birds
seeking a hiding place from man's inhumanity to earth,
from getting caught under
the grinding wheel of progress that keeps turning.
What is it to be a displaced bird
as the tractor tears through one's trusted home
of brush or felled tree?
How is it to fly anxiously to a harbor
for shelter instead of rest and relaxation
with a martini in hand?
The nest can be as treasured a place
as a house
with no mortgage attached
that will not sit empty if it is not paid for
two years after being built.

Robins, sparrows, thrushes, hawks.
How many birds are gypsies
that can move at the drop of a hat?
And how many humans
with all their heavy burden of belongings?
Is flying away as fanciful
as it is traumatizing?
What happens when the spirit wants to stay put
but the body must move?
What happens when the spirit
gets caught between coming and going?
What are the lifetime effects
of that margin?

Of Spring

The verdant trees
blooming
and every little bud
assuming
the passion of the branch
bursting
with joy for the petal
spinning.
Summer perches on the tips of feathers
stitching
nests of fresh mown grass together
breeding
each tiny heartbeat newly
stirring
the blood of all living things
pumping
from drops of rain there is
nurturing
of spring.

A Shatter of Wings. A Sonnet
Modoc County, California

Over the wide terrain fly the Sandhill Crane.
Into the distant hills bends the sky.
Around the chalky horizon do their graceful bodies frame
a circle of tundra grasses finely matted and dry.
A shatter of wings fans us gently from above
The call of the flock momentarily ours.
It shifts in harmonization, a surrender, a love
transposing the moments into hours.
Their voices fade to stillness, the stratosphere bows deep.
The sage brush hums a scented song for their passing.
Quiet estuary sleeps until the landing of webbed feet.
Two busts of feathers walk the marsh, faintly plashing.
  In this life we have found fortitude around the wilderness and its
instinctual cry.
  For woven in this way through the Sandhill Crane is that which will
never die.

Sandhill Crane: Migrate from Mexico in winter to the Arctic in summer
stopping in the tundra's of the western United States.
Plashing: a light splashing.

If I Hold You

If I hold you, not expecting anything
Even your arms
And I let go of the imposition of love
The heart will still answer
The call
Like geese flying north
Following the rugged mountains
Above swirling rivers.

Love, a wind

Love is like a fog you first see when the sun comes out.
It's there for just a little while, then it burns away. —Charles Bukowski

I saw how an old love
had blown past me like a wind last night
how he picked up his travel bag,
an old-fashioned boxy one
like the bag my uncle used to carry when he came down from Canada
to visit on the Amtrak Train,
turned to look one more time at my middle-aging face,
then got into his robin-egg blue flatbed truck
and drove slowly away
as if I would come running after
down a silent highway
where weeds grow around the dividing line,
crusty sagebrush blowing across the road, bats flitting in front of the
headlights,
and disappeared over a hill.

Do I occasionally think about that wind
how it blew and carried me with it for a while,
like a hurricane how it lifted me into its eye
knowing the wizard waited
to show me what lay past illumined longing?

The Swallows
For William

The swallows flit over us.
I sketch them as you watch.
Long tails sweep the ground, dark green backs,
a flash of white.
Snow Goose feathers cling to the scrub grass
where they group near the water
and the swallows weave, their tails following a magical lead
that I remember years ago
when we walked in Lincoln Park
hand-in-hand,
on Saturday mornings,
the swallows flitting around us over the green grass,
you in that pearl-button navy blazer,
me in my black beret.

Now here we are
in a remote corner of California
on the Pacific Flyway,
still nurtured by nature,
swallows still heralding
our spring.

After the Human Storm

As the dawn creeps into a solid mass
of chalk-white,
as the stillness of autumn breathes
in and out,
the leaves turning slowly
from forest-green to golden-brown,
the apples reddening
in a time of thwarted growth,
silent
meditative,
the summer second-homer's returned to the city,
lawnmowers stored,
fast boats gone,
owls hooting, bears dropping,
otters playing on wooden docks.
There is the calm
after the human storm.

When the coyote's walk
boldly the roads at night,
the wilderness returning to its source,
ducks gathering, huddling
at the bar.
These natural subjects to the world,
webbed and woven
beyond our limited sight,
steering a course toward the bend,
hesitant opening to the wide-open sea.

The old boat, lurching

The old boat is on its side again
beached
carpeted with mud and sand
tugged by the tide
bound by a rope to shore
tired of bearing its weight,
keeled.

For what purpose an old boat
on its knees
begging?
Once brandished (*by whom?*)
Coveted on mild summer nights (*when?*)

Time passing, time passing
high tide, boat floating yet snared
low tide, beached again
tide in, tide out
barnacles slowly attaching
detaching, their fleshy bodies dying
year after year.

Small boat, old boat—blue paint chipped white
yearning to be set adrift
to push with the wind
ride with a storm current
boards pealing loose
hull breaking in two
splintering,
rope
trailing.

Keeled: To capsize.

Red Clouds

For Uncle Raymond McKay

A red burst of clouds filled the sky tonight
and I knew my uncle's spirit was there
in a bright sweep of his Metis sash, high-stepping in a fast jig
between sipping a strong one
or at least a watered down one,
the best he could do
last December when we all
surprised him at his front door.

Like old times the party was made to order,
the fiddle music playing—Grand Rapids style—
as Uncle Ray called one then the other to get up and dance,
his tired breath casting him in his chair
to sit it out
as he watched us swing a partner—sister, mother or husband would
do.
And the spirit in his eyes, that *joie de vivre* from the heart,
was his gift to us that one last time.

Now the red clouds cascade south into infinity
as we walk briskly the evening lane
fast like he used to
and the red colors weave into scarlet
as he raises his glass, picks up the pace and waves
us one final good-bye.

Grand Rapids: Town in northern Manitoba, Canada.
Joie de vivre: Exuberant joy for life.

Upon a Farewell

Basho didn't know a thing about water
until he heard that frog. —Sam Hamill

It was not easy to be still; it was not easy to remain calm
when the Zen community keeled
after sitting graciously, oblivious
in the eye of a storm.
As the waves of transgression crashed over their insular stern,
silent outsider was my due recourse
from the ensuing gossip
      an unfortunate byproduct of the town.
But like the measured wake a boat makes
in the water,
rippling on until it laps
onto a land,
      for some lingering like distant white   waves on a reef far-off shore,
I learned to let go and within the flowing outward, within the fluidity
of time and change,
released the past onto the sand.
Now, as the particles may swirl and continue to settle,
      the pearls slowly growing again   inside the shell
and the hesitant truths of leaders, be they president, king or priest
are mirrored within the limitations of institution or military troop,
shaping into the simple spheres of human frailty,
turning, turning
like Yeats' widening gyres,
my call is yet
to be silent, to acknowledge all that is True
and upon a farewell to hear what is there
        in the rain softly tapping the windowpane
           in the swirl of the wind around the mountaintop
     in the swoosh of wheels on the wet roadway
in the determined cries of the Canada geese
              navigating north.

Distant white: A Japanese verse form that addresses something distant in
the mind but still lurking in the heart.

Alley-walking in Ashland. Some post-modern and not so modern thoughts
Oregon

Hills like
The hills curve gently into panorama's reminiscent of England,
Scotland or Wales
verdant light crisscrossing over the folds
of the earth
like a creased postcard
one has kept inside the inner leaf of a wallet
for several years,
some faint hint of the Old Country secured.
In town the light daintily settles on the brick walls
hinting of lonesome valleys beyond,
sparse, inhibited,
dotted with black-faced cattle,
rock fences edging over the hills,
the hills
that beckon the paintbrush,
the oils and the turpentine,
the wild rose
and that ancient rock's unyielding pose
like the curve of a dinosaurs back
standing in the impressionist's light with a purplish hue.

Alley-walking in Ashland
It's in the alleys.
It's in stepping between the upscale art gallery
and the back door,
wisteria hanging
around paint-chipped wooden gate.
It's when peeking into the shadowy
lawns at abandoned folding chairs
that blend into high grassy lawns
that haven't been mowed in weeks,
the smell of fresh baking bread
snaring the air.

These solo side-streets,
dirt lanes of the woebegone
untrammeled by all but the weekly garbage man
and occasional midnight cowboy
sneaking back from Jacksonville with a yawn,
they still hold a slow magic
like a Hawaiian island afternoon
of peach and pastel siding, porches open
to an old dog's brittle bone,
paw covering the eyes.

"The post-modern renegades." A vignette
The post-modern renegades
walk through town
their steps slow and even
scoping the earth
mildly unsettling the wind with their stares
a couple of plain-clothes tribesmen
appearing then disappearing
like surreal images duplicated in an Andy Warhol western façade
while the fashionably casual
busy past
fanning around the invisible wave
as the renegade cast goes by.
The renegades shift
in broad daylight, shaping into a dreamscape against orange poppies
backdrop of velvet-brown hill
a hard-lipped sun at their backs,
shading their potent stares
with short-brimmed hats.
Up the alleyway they drift
on quick feet
like coyotes
donned for flight.

Oh, for the lack of heat and flies
A Pantoum

I've never been as tired of a month as I am of this July
The endless days check off slowly in mental time
That Independence Day photo on the calendar has gotten so dry
Oh, for the lack of heat and flies.

The endless days check off slowly in mental time
The sun beating down, a constant 'why'
Oh, for the lack of heat and flies
I've never prayed so anxiously for a month to go by

The sun beating down, a constant 'why'
I dream of autumn slipping in on the sly
and have never prayed so anxiously for a month to go by.
May this weather pattern whither, brown leaves kiss summer good-bye.

I dream of autumn slipping in on the sly
I've never been as tired of a month as I am of this July
May this weather pattern whither, brown leaves kiss summer good-bye
That Independence Day photo on the calendar has gotten so dry.

What is this thing called mystical? Glimpses of Jack Kerouac

each rain-drop contains
> *infinite universes of*
> *existence the essence*
>> *of which is undisturbed light.*
>>> *—Jack Kerouac,*
>>> *"Some of the Dharma"*

Why was he so drawn by the sensory call of the city
to a Skid Row hotel room, chafing,

> when the Truth had presented so vividly
> like a babe uttering first words, mystical revelations
> pouring
from his mouth in his musings with Hozomeen

amidst "stark naked rock, pinnacles and thousand feet high
protruding...timbered shoulders"[1] ?

Why did he race down the mountain,
tearing his feet in pathetically thin canvas shoes

> to make the boat that would
> take him away
from his mystic's nest in the clouds?

Why did Kerouac keep falling off the mountain

tumbling into Chinatown or Times Square,
> cigarette butt burning into
a thumbnail moon,

thoughts racing like jukebox tracks
> the old pack of maniacs running alongside?

> Who is this guy Kerouac, wondered I,

who charged through stream-of-consciousness cants,
          rants
and not-so-well-written Buddhist chants?

          A dope fiend
          like my mother used to call guys like him?

An unsuspecting carouser of the unconscious?

          What can he teach about *Self*?
          Beyond drunk self, sober self, alone self, crowded self—
"Get on board self
          the freight train is a-moving!"

Lone beat-friend, playing
                    sweat-cool tongue-rips off your saxophone-loaded
vision,

          consider the sky, Mr. Kerouac, how tightly-wrapped
          the universe can appear to be
in a nutshell.

[1] From *Desolation Angels*. 1965, p. 3

Gang Leader, Hummingbird Feeder

Gang Leader

After being a gang leader
in Chicago in the 1930's
he stayed hollow and hard inside
the turf defended
too many times,
the baseball bats, the fists,
the running outnumbered
taking the first blow
because he was in charge
when they rumbled
with the Serbian gangs
bulked-up on false notions
of pride,
who broke the rules
by carrying clubs.
His edge was living
lean and mean.

Still, to be beaten
was to be a coward in his mind,
so anger defined him.
It was the only emotion
he could survive,
that fear of not fearing,
carelessly not caring,
the forces of the city
calling his name.

Later, he funneled his anger
into the precision of machine work
shoving aside the family years
beating any tender inclinations
into a callous pulp.
Discipline, after all,
was what had carried him on the street.

Hummingbird Feeder

On an old-age morning
a hummingbird claims
the air tufts
above the rose bushes
in his wife's garden,
its bright feathers
whirring
like fruit in a blender
and he unfolds the newspaper
at the kitchen table,
looks up and watches
as two fight for the territory
of a blood-red rose
despite the thorns.

That day he buys
a feeder
at the Walmart,
starts to lure them
with water and sugar
mixed regularly
by his dogged assistance
to quick-moving birds
defending their turf,
knowing the forces of the city
are part of their game,
that fear of not fearing
carelessly not caring
seeking turf rights in a bird feeder,
an instinctual knowledge
about when to hone in and fly back out.
Discipline, he figured, was what carried them
to his street.

The California Dream is Dead
Let's protect the California Dream for all Californians! —Arnold Schwarzenegger

The California Dream is dead.
It is headed south on the lap of a trucker
on his way to LA to drop off a load,
heavy,
refuel then drive north, east, even west
to China.
The clutch shifts downward, knocking.
Like the grocery clerk tossing another dime
into an empty palm
he's seen days,
at least heard of them,
dreamed of them,
of a two-acre parcel of land, a car and a house.

Get your programs here. Win a car and a house.

Did he know
what was hiding
under the sweet-smiling
fine-print, 'sign here quick' reminders,
the liability of job-loss recession.

Foreclosure! Repossession! We now have your car and your house.

The mountain sits primly
like a bird in a gilded cage.
Down the street smug yuppie shoppers
carry lattes in stylishly gloved hands,
platinum hair ruffling in the wind.
It's another upscale California town,
complacent, cozy, cliquish, giving to the poor
via the Internet
the same dream
vying for cover.
For the cage is breaking down now, the birds fluttering about inside
afraid to fly, to share seed with the

sorely-assisted neighbor
they've been helping for years
to stay on the dole.

The California dream has been dead
for a long time. Did it ever live and breathe?
Did it ever sink into the suffocated soil? Or did it always roll off
like a mega-house on an eroded hillside, built on a surface loam
spilling into the sea?

Get your programs here. Win a car and a house. [Fade-out]

With chalk

I did have a few years with chalk
even though I always worried the dust would get on my jackets and
skirts
branding me as 'teacher'
when I trudged down the hallway
and climbed onto the city bus for the long ride home.

I did have a few years
before the onslaught of iPods, texting and Facebook,
(and online teaching)
when a classroom had more blackboard than computer to help jiggle
thoughts
from inquisitive minds,
before curiosity was dimmed by screen glare
and the classroom became a cyber room
no longer filled with breathing bodies,
who laughed or stared or even pinioned me with expressions of "Who
cares."

I did have time to reach students face to face,
to think out loud, to speak,
before Tweet, before the Internet
made cheat a five-letter word
(and teacher a photograph, five years old)
and reading lists didn't make student avatar's yawn
and the instruction hour became more and more fluid until an isolated
desk gave way
to a table at a café
(amongst strangers).

I did have a chance to show students
how to sit in a circle and listen
to each other share
before they slid behind a virtual curtain
(and I did too)
and body language was demoted to the ancient archives of the
handwritten.

I did have the opportunity once
to hold a piece of chalk between my fingers and to lift it to the
blackboard,
the dust settling upon my jacket cuff and then on my skirt on its drift
to the floor.

In a glacier known as the heart
For Chihiro Inoki, Mt. Shasta, California

The meeting with the goddess (who is incarnate in every woman) is the final test of the talent of the hero. —Joseph Campbell.

In a glacier known as the heart
she missed a step and fell 1500 feet down
down
an icy gulch, sacrificing her femininity to rocks, deadly instruments
of family grief, imprinting the knowledge that adventure
for a woman today can mean plummeting down the steeple of a
mountain
down,
while two men watch.

What had frozen in two men
as they stood and watched in horror
a woman
slide down a glacier
her talent, her energy, her intelligence unable to stop
the trail of her life
as it wisped behind her like a ghostly veil?

Did either man know, alone or together
on this, the last journey of a woman's life,
a man's protective instinct; that an arm, surely two, could have reached
out
to catch a woman's body before her trip became a fall?
Had their link to the hero vanished
decades, even a century ago, their sense of male duty,
their intuitive knowing
about a woman's fear
only manifesting when they clambered down the mountain
to try to save her
after she'd died?

Did she expect them to be heroes
when she first scaled the peak, assumed they realized

that hidden behind her intent to be brave,
like one of the guys,
was a truly feminine fear?

And in the slow seconds after her foot slipped
and the ice carried her like rapids,
the rocks snatching her,
hurling her into a mother's womb,
her father's head shaking,
did she meet them at last at an archetypal place,
of male and female,
goddess and hero,
in a glimpse of the ancient,
beyond incarnate?

Swath of red

What's greater, Pebble or Pond? —Theodore Roethke

The Red-winged Blackbirds
have taken to the tops of the alder trees,
singing in chorus,
readying their lungs for the great symphony
of a coming spring.
Down the road they perch atop the cattails
harmonizing
while the geese
nest in the rushes.
The Mallards have been breeding for weeks.
My body gains a little more energy each day
in between rests,
my form a Georgio de Chirico mannequin
on a cubist canvas
(no less appropriate for the Louvre)
with a particular splash of vivid color—bright green, yellow,
a swath of red for the scar.
I shall not select the royal blue.
I will use the bright yellow.

Few understand how it is not to mourn
a missing breast
in a society of constant cleavage.
How it is not
to mind one appendage of female allure
instead of two.

Does the body not drop away when we die?
What is there when we deeply sleep?

And the Red-winged Blackbirds,
the swath of red
most visible at the peak of song,
are here for the duration.

Telephone Booth Blues. Singing
Based upon US West Coast telephone booth photographs

Essential phone-beat
on a hot day, lonely stretch of road,
unglued calls.

A barren hill rears ruggedly through the glass
like a Stegosaurus pausing.
Telephone ringing, a specter's call.

Pink telephone collage
abstract portrait of yesterday's communication
splashes the corner lot with sing-song ardor.

A shadow in time, captured in a still-frame with cars.
Doors eternally open
Receiver of nothing.

A verbal portal assisting pleasure
when the surf is up.
Willing to stand by.

Castaway bus-station booth
at the far side of consequences.
Still helping spin new tales for the ride.

What did it hold once
fashioned by tears, the fabric
of an old-fashioned road house stop.

To call anywhere is to be anywhere
foggy street or harbor town
on an ocean-swept morning.

Long stretch of highway, a fixture
in broad daylight.
Invisible receptacle of coins by night.

Empty vessels like modern-day ships
passed on traveler's time.
Under a grey sky at noon.

Accessory to a tourist's street
like a mod model on a 1960's stage
wisps of stolen conversation memorized in the midst.

Performer of magic—hollow voice
threaded to the end of a box-line.
What mood does it present?

An expansive station booth
to carry vocal wishes over water,
dappled by shifting sunlight.

Resting the eyes where sky meets land
longing for home or truth.
It is in the calling.

Telephone booth blues
singing
still giving voice to wild wants
over quick-stop beers.

London Slices

I wander through each chartered street,
Near where the chartered Thames does flow,
And mark in every face I meet,
Marks of weakness, marks of woe. —*William Blake*

Morning sunlight slices the walls
while the city awakens slowly
drags its feet out of bed
in the bitter cold. The Tube thunders
dutifully under our partial-basement room.
Sheep are dying in the late winter freeze
up north. We offer merit as the heater toasts our bones.
I cancel the visit to an old friend near Northumberland
dissolving the decision about the elite fast train versus the slow
pauper's bus.
Bundling up in scarves, hats and thermal wear
we trundle through the empty park to stretch our legs
an occasional vodka bottle tossed
by a last night reveler the only sign of squalor
on the affluent dog-walkers green.

Piccadilly no longer exists
as it was.
Rows of fine shops and eateries have re-formed the circus.
We find a meager establishment, stools facing out,
serving spring rolls, saffron rice, baguettes and tea.
Perplexed by all of the prosperously fashionable, aloof
in their haute couture, I superimpose their images with that of
Romaine Brooks, circa 1920's, steely in her black hat and white gloves
on the same London sidewalk in the afternoon.
"Nobody can afford London anymore…except the rich," our cabbie
spouts
en route to the airport. He appeals to us through
his rear-view mirror. We commiserate about all those places
now unaffordable, unattainable to but some
and he gives us an American thumbs-up as we exit his cab.
We marvel once more over the Dickensian chimneys
before they disappear below the clouds.

The Alentejo
Portugal

The Alentejo
The Alentejo
region of higher dreams and Old World visions
asking for nothing
giving
in return
in the fading light of an Atlantic sea coast day
along the esplanade
lingering, arm-in-arm
over the cobbled streets
cast of uneven, patterned brick squares

And the sun-softened old faces
And the kindly curious stares
And the golden-grained sand
sifting through the fingers
in this transported world
Obrigado, Thank you
Obri-ga-do

The Alentejo
The Alentejo
where the wind blows in the early morning
across the land, through the eucalyptus trees
the cork trees, the olive trees
shifting
Where hard work is simply work
and the café is firstly for conversation and second for coffee
a place to meet old friends, day after day
A place to meet
The camaraderie of men rising with the cigarette smoke
Freely puffing
Masculine jaws, wide-shouldered, vocal
Old, young
chatting, laughing, commenting on the people
who pass

And the taxi drivers
And the taxi drivers
skillfully maneuvering the narrow streets
the winding country roads between the Alentejo and there
winning the passengers trust
without seat belts
Trust
in their bare hands
in their hairpin turns
in the dexterity beyond daring

The Alentejo
The Alentejo
White-washed houses
trimmed with red, blue, yellow, green
red-tiled roofs
against the sky
on a clear day, the clouds drifting
And the storks nesting
on telephone poles
Stork nests lodged in the forks of transmitter towers
Storks circling wider and wider overhead
to the tinkling bells of cows
the soft blue eyes of donkeys blinking
under the tree that holds the cuckoo's post
swallows swinging past

The Alentejo
The Alentejo
Transported world across the Atlantic sea
Obrigado

Of the Snake River Canyon, once again I am thinking

Of the creased land, pressed permanently into folds,
the sharp edges chiseled into view
from an airplane window
while the Snake River twists solidly,
holding space, beckoning nothing,
not fantasy, not refuge.
It is but a water basin, moving.

The Snake River Canyon, an image
in freed moments
in late-afternoon light,
a landscape in brown and rose-pink
with dark, sapphire string.
A message of remoteness seen
from a jet's eye
passing over once, slowly.
The stillness, the quiet
appealing
for miles
distant.

On the horizon
Sequim, Washington

It's a Sunday after
noon
and the tides are low on the beaches,
seagulls plucking through the muck for clam and crab
and the sky so high
mackerel clouds are pulled taught into a dusty dome,
ducks waddling forth to plop onto the sand,
partnered pairings following each other's tails.
And Canada across the strait. Does it beckon?

The heron's mindfully wading the shallows,
the water curling,
not quite catching the quicksteps of the sandpipers.
Broken shells trail where the water stopped before receding,
rocky outcrops carved between licks of sand.
And the island in the distance. Does it beckon?

The air, sharp and clear,
the scents of seaweed mingling with a burst of hydrangea
blown in from a nearby garden,
drift logs chiseled and worn, long detached from the living tree,
the horizon big and wide like Montana with seascape.
And the vacant table at the city sidewalk café in the morning sunlight.
And the cool, shadowy porch on a friendly street in a small town.
And the lonely roadway winding along the Pacific Ocean at dusk.
And the sense of knowing it is all the same place.

Shaniko, Oregon. Population 25

There is the dimming twilight
upon a toss of buildings,
upon a ghostly town of the past-tense
amidst the rolling wheat lands,
soon to become another layer of humanity,
the graves of ancients.

Streets empty, windows staring darkly out,
café closed for decades, door
closed tight, red and orange tints of sunset
framing spare, wooden structures in silhouette.
Relics.

Camera in hand, a tourist walks,
trying to hold the town
before it fades.
Wind whipping, dirt-dust swirling,
long-ago hovering in the floorboards, in the paint-stripped
sidings.

Breathing in the old air
before, after the twilight
and the town disappears
behind, along a ribbon-road.
Haunting.

We Return her Home
Grand Rapids, Manitoba, 2015

We had been planning it for weeks,
for months. In fact she had set it to paper 15 years before.
That she wanted her ashes buried in both the United States
and Canada.
In Seattle where she lived with Dad for 66 years, and in Grand Rapids,
the town she still called home.

At the airport, on the US side, we are ready
to take her there, one last time.
Her urn tucked inside a carry-on bag, her last wishes answered
on the wind.
We, flying over farmlands, over prairies,
rivers coursing below, rapids churning,
the names of the towns and cities changing to Cree and French:
Nipawin, Beausejour.
Minnedosa, The Pas.

Later, a stretch of highway heads north from Winnipeg,
farmland gives way to short trees and brush.
This is the stage of the Raven
and the Prairie Chicken.
Beyond the 59th Parallel
where dirt roads shoot into the tundra, into infinity.

When we sit down at the town café
news about our arrival spreads fast.

Many gather to honor her, a last elder's return.
And the prayers, the hymns are recited, sung heartily at her request.

Outside, we fling sweet grass, a handful of dirt atop her urn
secured by a fresh pine box.
All pay their respects
with a handshake, a hug
and we exit quietly. Quietly we mourn.

Early the next day,
we stand one last time
by her side. The birds sing mightily in the trees,
the sunshine cascades over the ancient gravestones, over the roses,
grandfather holds her once again in his arms.
We have returned her home.

Harvest Moon, Eclipsing
Spokane, WA

As the Harvest Moon eclipses,
we stand in awe in the parking lot
on a hill, facing east, a small group of caregivers and ones in care.
The moon turns a rose-red, the aura dimmed by city lights
and a slip of a woman named Alice,
her hands in pockets, wool hat pulled over her ears,
wonders if she'll see the next, in 19 years. "I'll be 100" she says, wistful.
She brightens, telling us about a green moon
she saw from the boardwalk in Atlantic City, New Jersey
when she was 16-years-old, how the climactic conditions
were somehow just right
to create the unusual color—green
as the moon hung over the ocean.

And Tom—the care giver of old Bill who sings Karaoke as breath
therapy
from his wheelchair studio—jogs up and greets each of us like family
with a warm hug.
He tells us, "The eclipse is an act of God!" He raises his hands
to the sky, his ex-wife's name tattooed on his forearm. Then runs
inside
to fix Bill's dinner.

Ben, a quiet middle-aged man in a checkered wool jacket, wheels his
mother over. He is hasty. She is missing her shoes, her white hair
disheveled.
They look up at the sky.
Patiently we wait for a last patch of light to disappear,
but the lower right corner of the moon does not darken to shadow.
Maybe it is our proximity,
the New Jersey woman and I
speculate. The moon may appear more eclipsed elsewhere in the world
like in Africa.
Somewhere far from this parking lot
where another slice of humanity
stands together in awe

of this thing outside the usual,
of this,
in the roar of the expressway,
in the face of getting old,
in the face of Spiritus Mundi,
in the face of a rose-red moon
in the face of.

Spiritus Mundi: World Spirit. A Latin term used by WB Yeats to describe the collective soul of the universe.

After the Paris atrocities
November 13, 2015

There has been a sense that nothing is right
with the world for quite some time.
That human bedlam has been subtly insinuating
itself despite the attempts
at make-believe, at cover-up, at plasticizing.
And what about the murdering of the innocents?
What century after century
keeps placing them in the path of the self-righteous?

I want to sit in a Paris café
and pray.
I want to watch the day
dawn there
and the night slide back
like a wolf creeping into its den.
I want to watch the city wake up.
Wake up.

I want to sit past the death
and the decay,
the oppression and isolation,
the poverty and wary purpose,
lack of water and lack of heat,
food, decrepitude,
religiosity and secularism,
enlightened ones and unenlightened ones,
and time.

Time.
I want to sit past time
as the sun blinks its eyes open,
and walk to the Eiffel Tower
and look up.

The Patterning of Leaves

It is the primeval time of morning
when the light silhouetting the leaves
is a pale yellow above the horizon
and the abundant foliage can fool you
into believing it will never stop growing again.

Only there is something in the patterning of the leaves
something known
in dream or not-dream.

A distant bird cavorting above the tree tops,
then gone.

At the Town Café

This present moment   that lives on   to become   long ago. —*Gary Snyder*

1

The snow is receding, the icicles having dropped.
The café is crowded with those who before, dared not venture outside,
dared not slip on the ice.
Like the owl who has spotted the vole
they are focused,
sweeping down upon their moments.

Across the street there is the brick apartment building. I search the top,
left window
and find a Siamese cat poised inside on the sill, one paw up, licking.
A tiny lip of snow dangles from the roof, drips.

There is room for silence amidst the hubbub.
There is room for the wooden chair
at the door, vacant.
The fixed play of the bored workers does not stain it.
Yet the café does not ring with clarity.
It is simply calm in a steady, drone-like way,
a way that invites the floor boards to creak.

2

Some places are more like home in the fixed spaces of memory.
A certain back stairs, a porch,
a kitchen to the left, a window opening to the right,
a road outside. The trees turning,
the big chairs facing out,
old conversations drifting.

3

A young boy sits at the window with the cat;
the cat is now a tabby. He pets the cat as I watch far below in the
crowded café.
Snow swirls between us, silence. He gets up and now it is only the cat
at the window and me down below watching
from across the street. Other people, their shadows, cross behind.

The silence of the snowfall exists between us,
between me, the cat, the café and the shadow people who move behind
the cat in the room.
The cat has held its reign at the window
and is drawn by something inside the warm apartment that I cannot
see.
I continue to look
at the snow, at the wrought iron chairs piled one into the other in the
patio, at the tables turned upside down picking up snow, at the snow
melting.

The cat's face appears from a corner of the window then disappears. It
is playing tricks upon the mind while the snow silently swirls.
Down the sidewalk across the street from the Corinthian columns
is an empty bench.
The snow is getting wetter.
A fire truck goes by slowly; the pavement swishes with wet snow
beneath the wheels.
I think of a painting
by Charles Demuth, *The Figure 5 in Gold.* Then the fire truck and the
thought of the painting are gone.
The cat does not return to the window.
The bench down the street is empty.

4
A jet airplane tilts around the brick building across the street.
Rain patters on the wet pavement.
Birds are lined up on the telegraph wires.
I watch the birds lift up and circle the grey, chalky sky. A smattering
of them gather on the ledge near the top of the building.
Below is a line of windows that look they were done by Edward
Hopper
for his painting, *Early Sunday Morning.*
There is no sign of a cat. There are no dogs either.
The wrought iron fence surrounding the patio is jeweled with drops of
water.
The café is one pace. Attempts to speed it up come to a full stop.
The people in the café appear two dimensional, pasted onto the
foreground like a suburban lawn.

A freight train rolls along the track around the corner and out of town.
The black silhouette of a cat appears in the left upper window and
soon disappears.
The rain has stopped.
A steel grey jaguar drives by.
The rain has created a wet sheen on the chair seats and table tops
outside the window.
A barista with a high-pitched voice, tone-deaf, disturbs the café's tenor.

5
Everything and nothing changes at the café.
People meet. They talk. They enjoy the sight of a black, Labrador dog
with white whiskers on his muzzle, who looks into the window
from outside. He, who only wants the eye, the touch of his master, to
anticipate a romp away from the circle of faces through the window.

The people are youthful or try to look that way. They are affluent
or try.
It is a cloudy Saturday, a type of day when the café fills with chatter,
with relief
that the week is over and it is time to play.
At the next table two children sit with their electronic tablets
like adults, heads tucked over their screens, brows furrowed, the child's
way shunned
by their parents, by themselves.

Sweets are lined up like temptresses inside the counter near the café
entrance.
Outside, and around the wall that separates,
the cat sits in the upper corner window to the far left.
A mirage, a changeling.
It licks its paw.
One need not see to know
it is there.

6
The sun is dappling a calico cat who sprawls on the windowsill
in the upper far corner
warming with the rising temperature.

Its face is a white mask and there are spots of white on its body that
flash on and off with movement.
A green canvas awning cover flaps with a mild wind.
The sky is watercolor blue and bone white,
a stratosphere with cloud.

It is an open and shut sort of day at the café,
heated conversations running full steam,
the espresso bar roaring fast.
The sunshine *is* the weather.
It brightens a large swath of the floor.

The number twenty bus waits to pass at the stop light outside.
The top is painted lime-green, the color of mechanized equipment and
graphic design.
The clouds move, the café moves
with the passing morning.
It is day
then it is night.
I consider the café after closing,
after darkness,
the cat looking out the window above, in the far corner,
at the city.
The vacant streets below.

Made in the USA
San Bernardino, CA
23 July 2017